Renee farmer

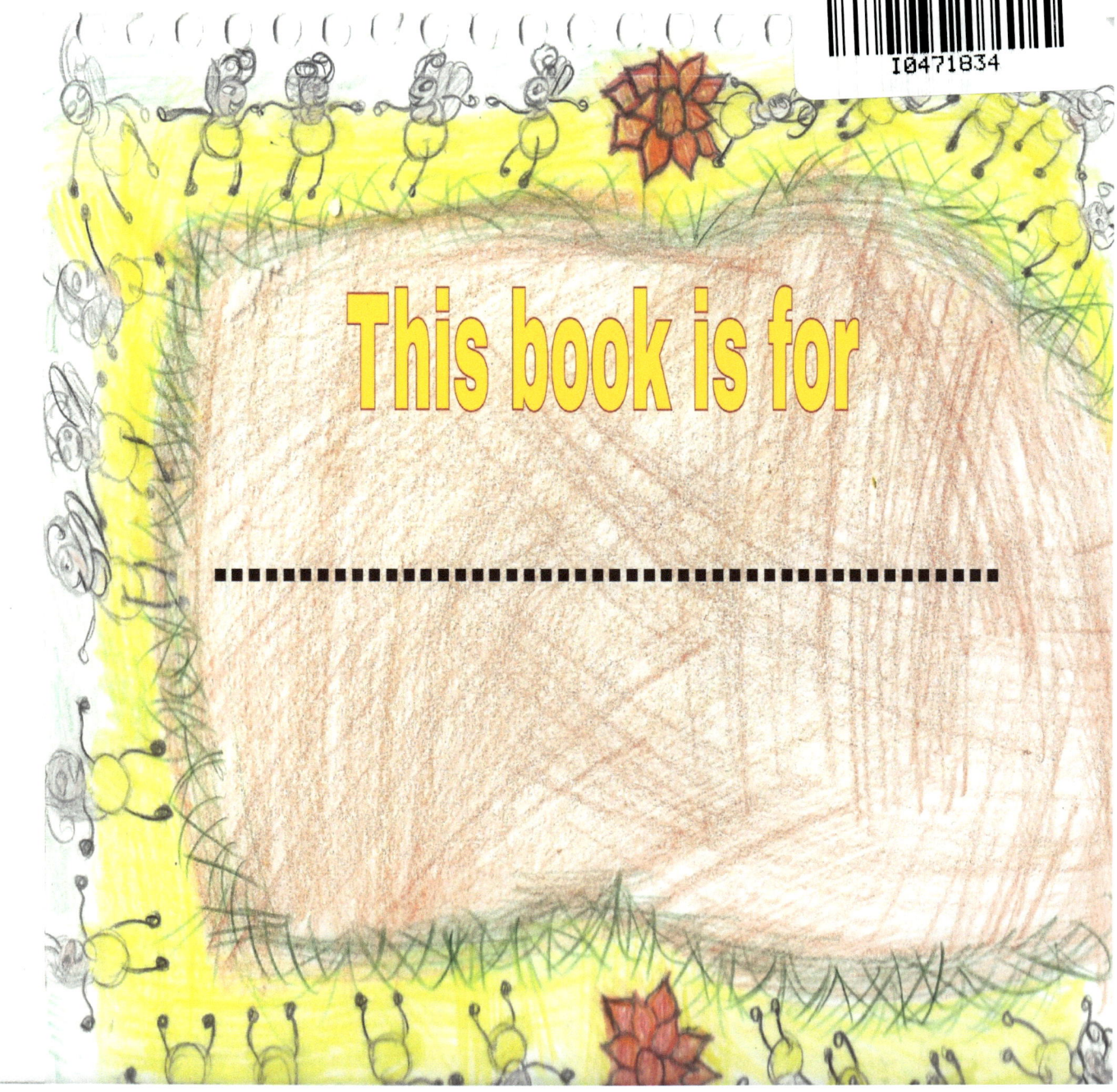

This book is for

....

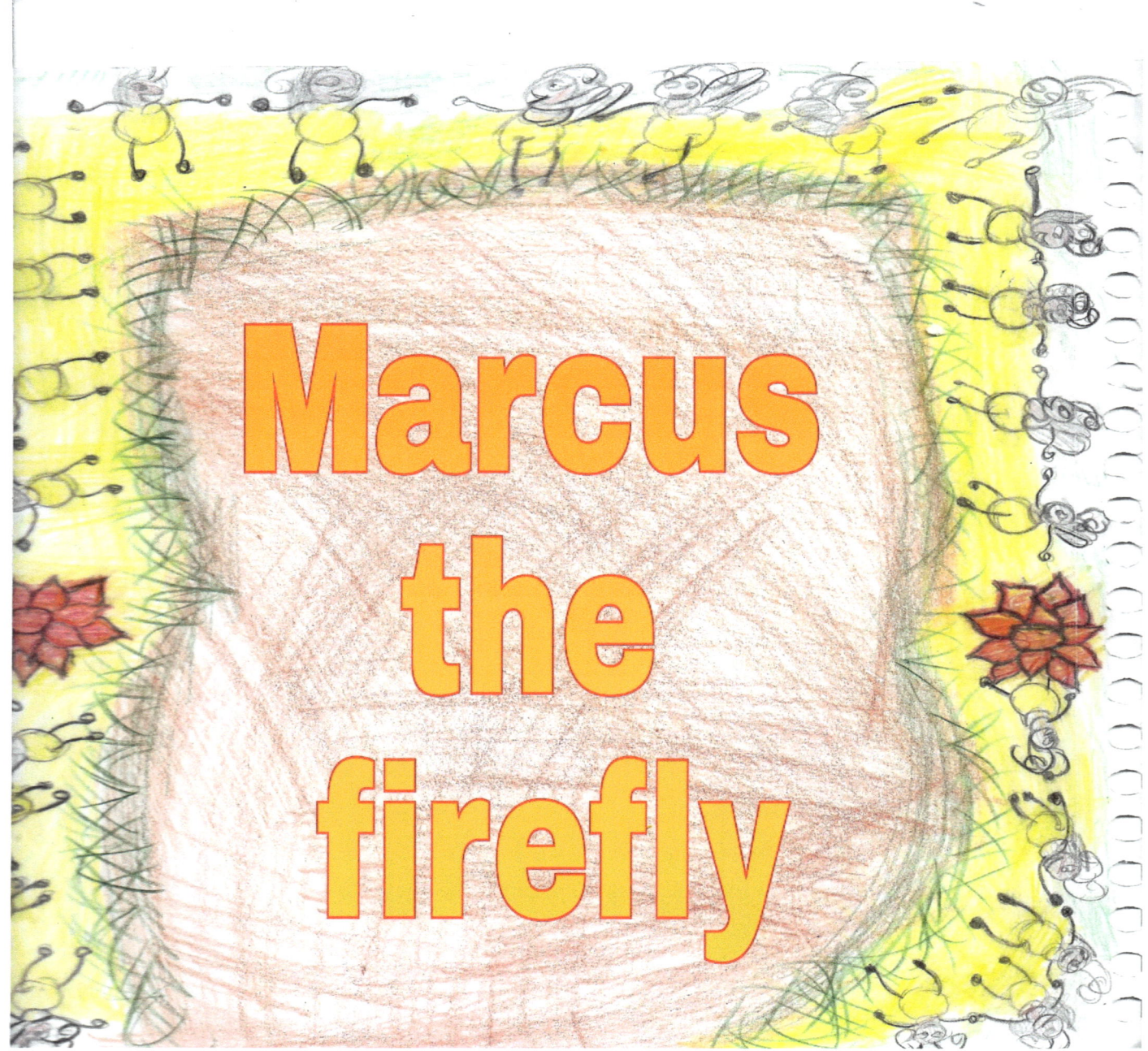

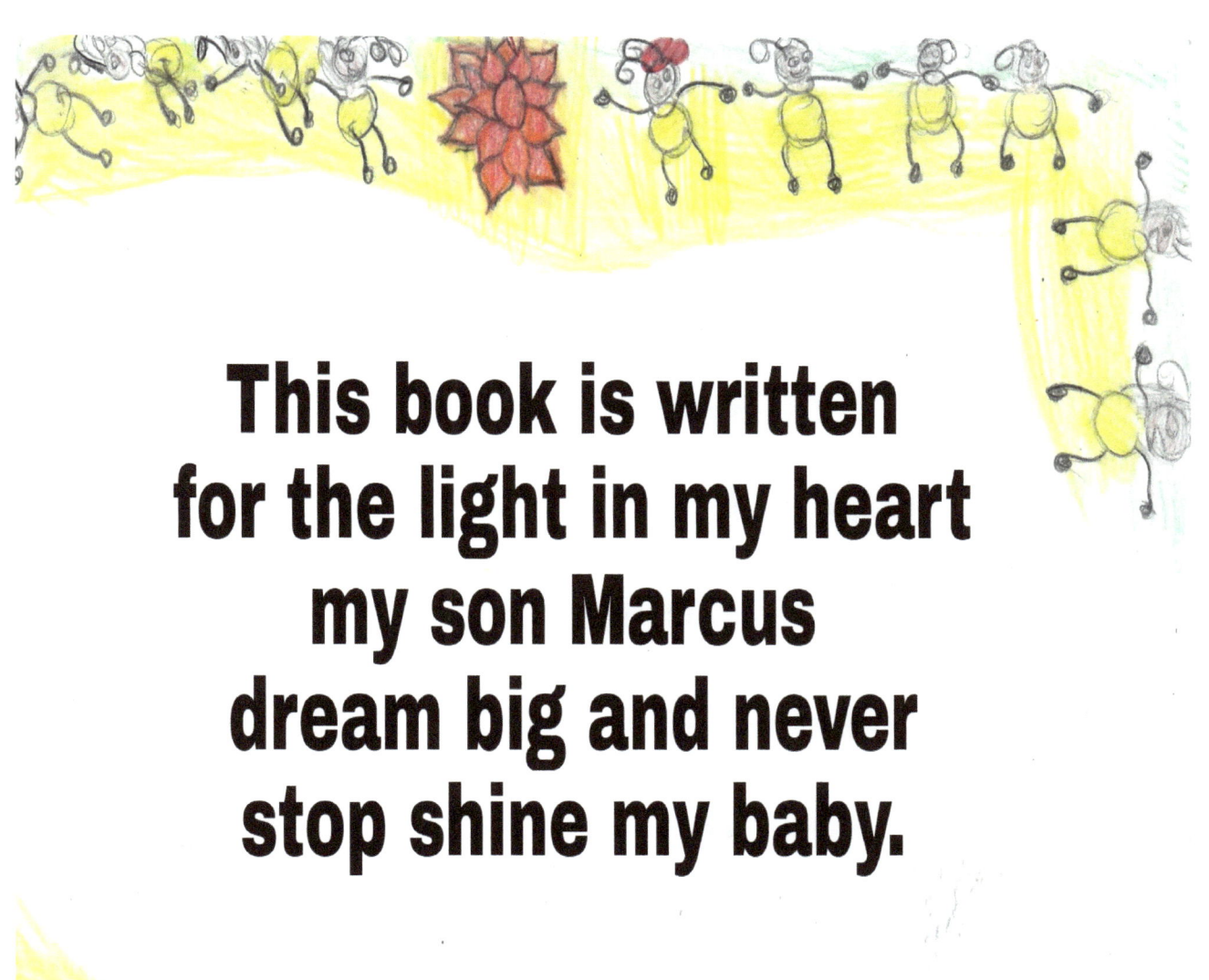

This book is written
for the light in my heart
my son Marcus
dream big and never
stop shine my baby.

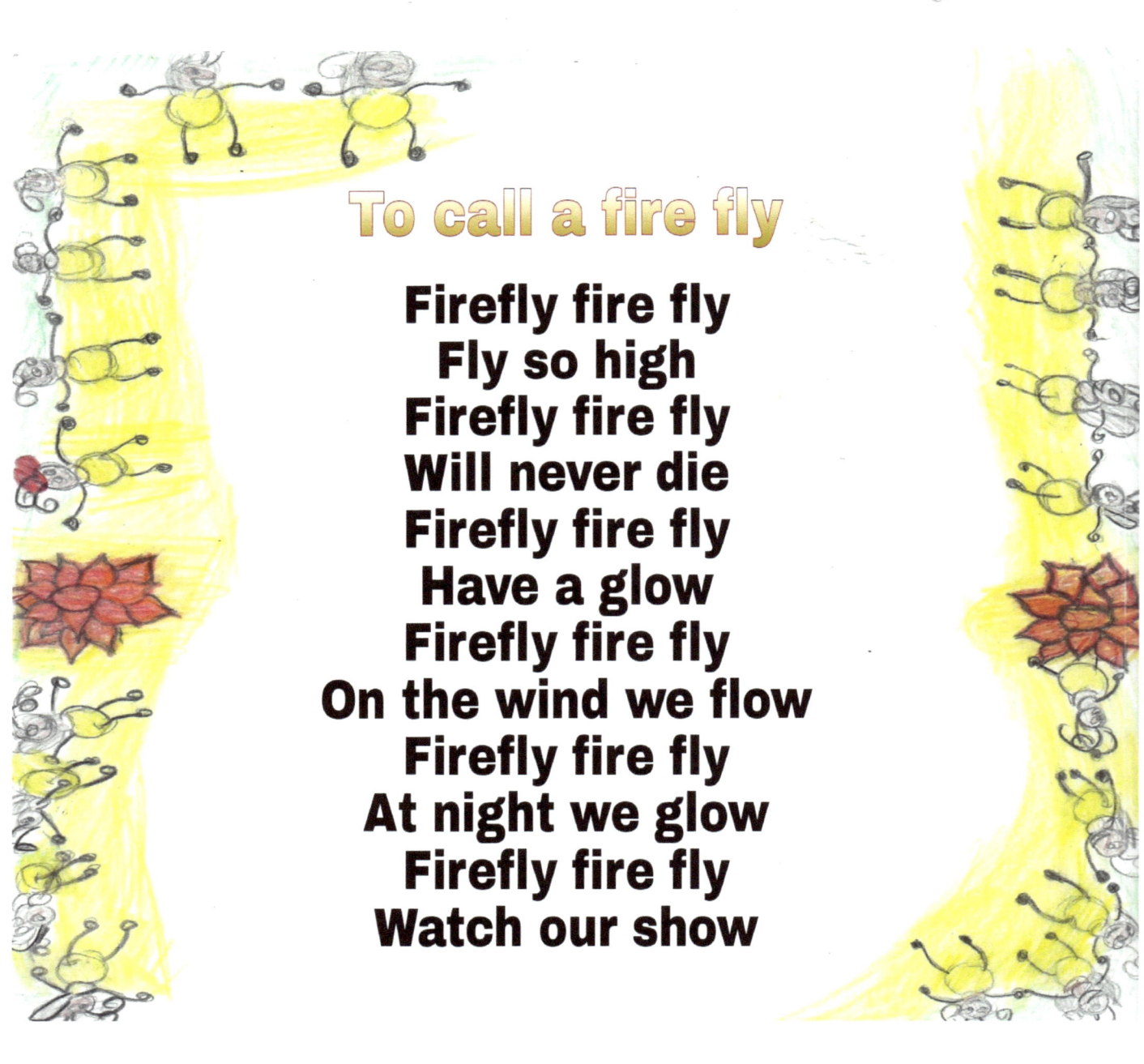

To call a fire fly

Firefly fire fly
Fly so high
Firefly fire fly
Will never die
Firefly fire fly
Have a glow
Firefly fire fly
On the wind we flow
Firefly fire fly
At night we glow
Firefly fire fly
Watch our show

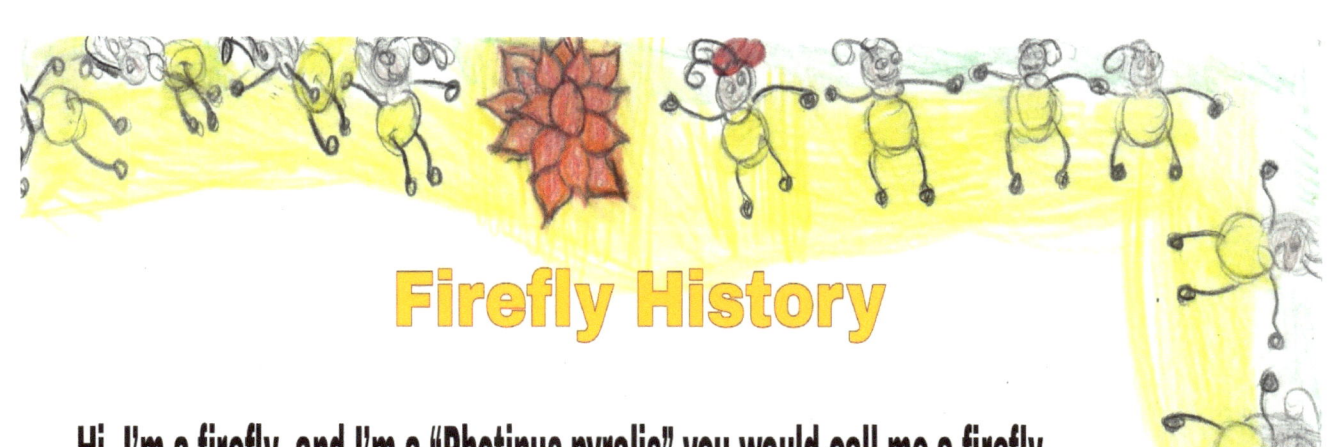

Firefly History

Hi, I'm a firefly and I'm a "Photinus pyralis" you would call me a firefly.

You know the little lighting bugs you like to capture in a glass jar on a cool spring night.

Yes, that is us and some helpful facts about fire flies some of us are seen at night.

A baby firefly is called a glow worm that is what I am and I mostly eat plants.

I produce a light green glow but not like Uncle Run.

Adult fire flies have a yellowish glow.

Uncle Run likes to eat pollen that's the thick yellow stuff inside flowers.

They eat slugs it sounds so delicious.

We have over 200 different kinds of fire flies all over the world.

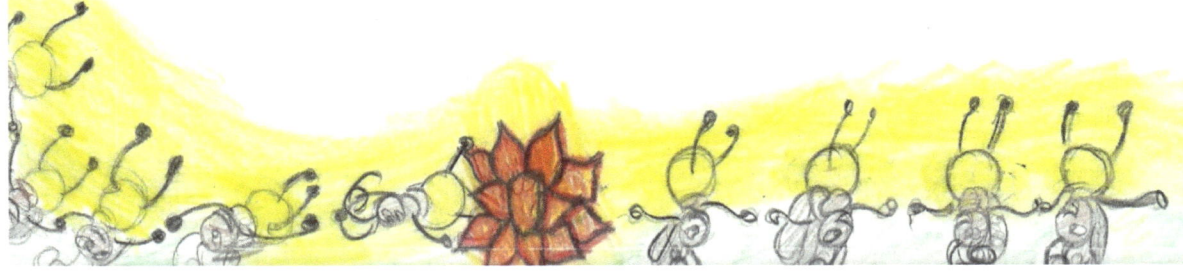

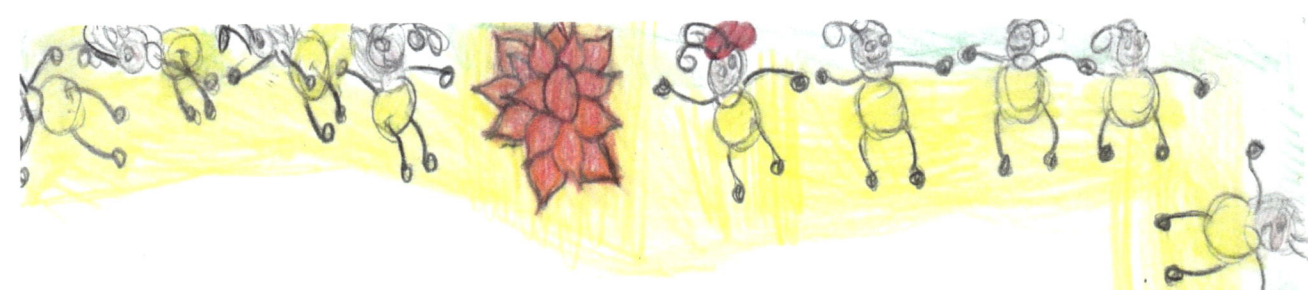

I am called a nocturnal insect but the others go out in the day light like birds.
For self defense the ones that fly in the day taste funny nasty.
So the predators learn to avoid them.
We flash our light to communicate from a distance.
If captured for our beautiful light to glow on dark nights.
Please let us go when you finish so you can see our light show.

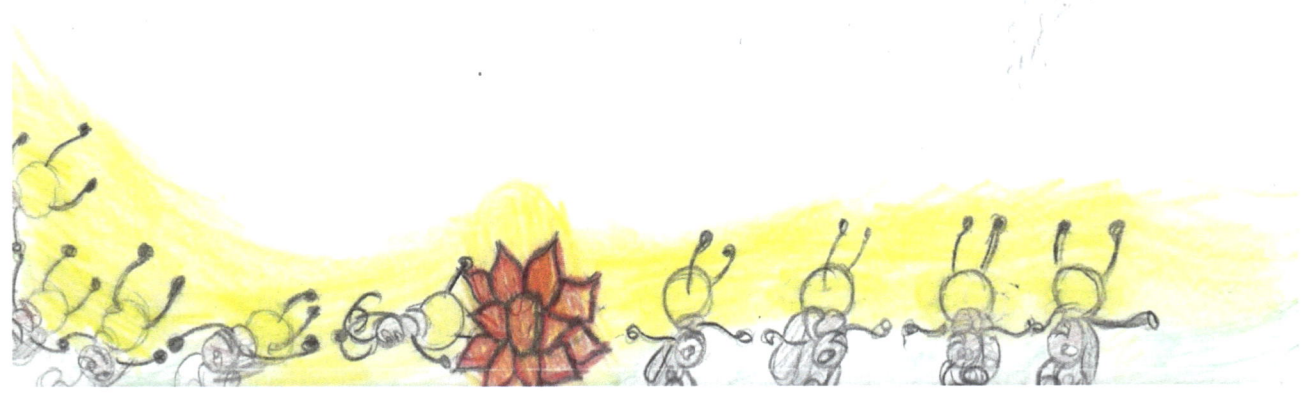

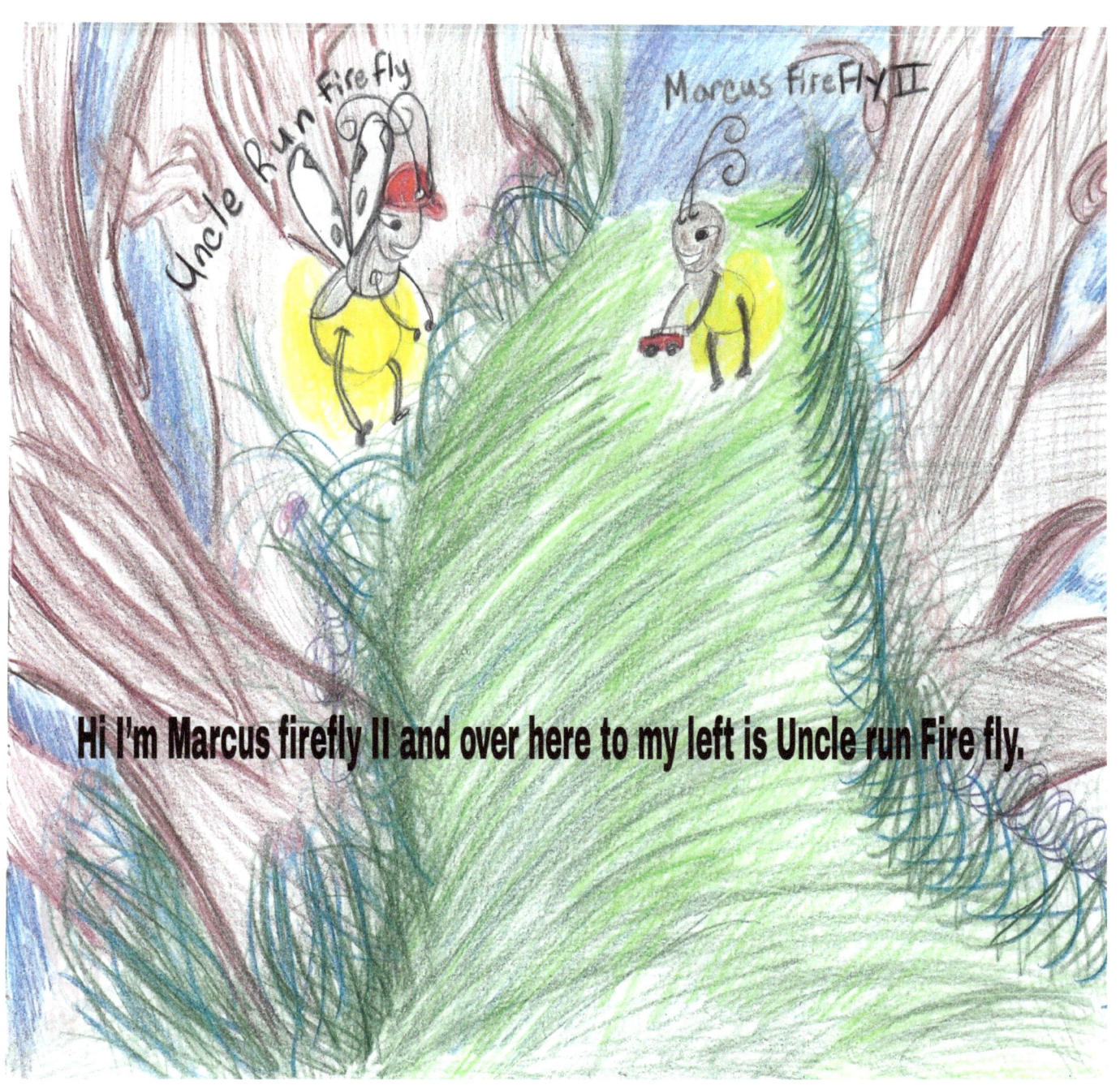

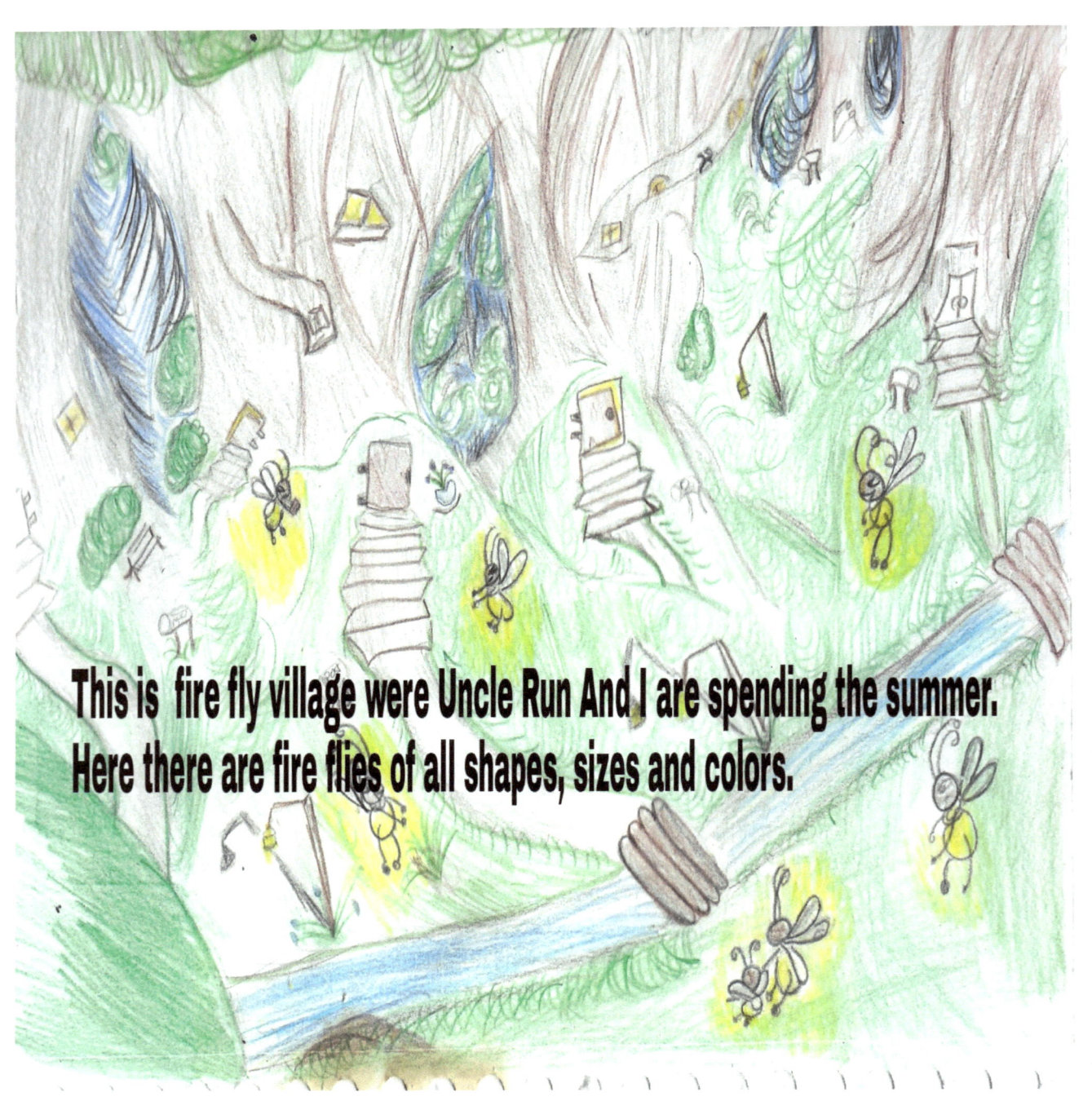

This is fire fly village were Uncle Run And I are spending the summer.
Here there are fire flies of all shapes, sizes and colors.

This is my first camp fire where we sang "Call of the fire fly" song.
It is so amazing.
How all the different fire flies glimmer together.

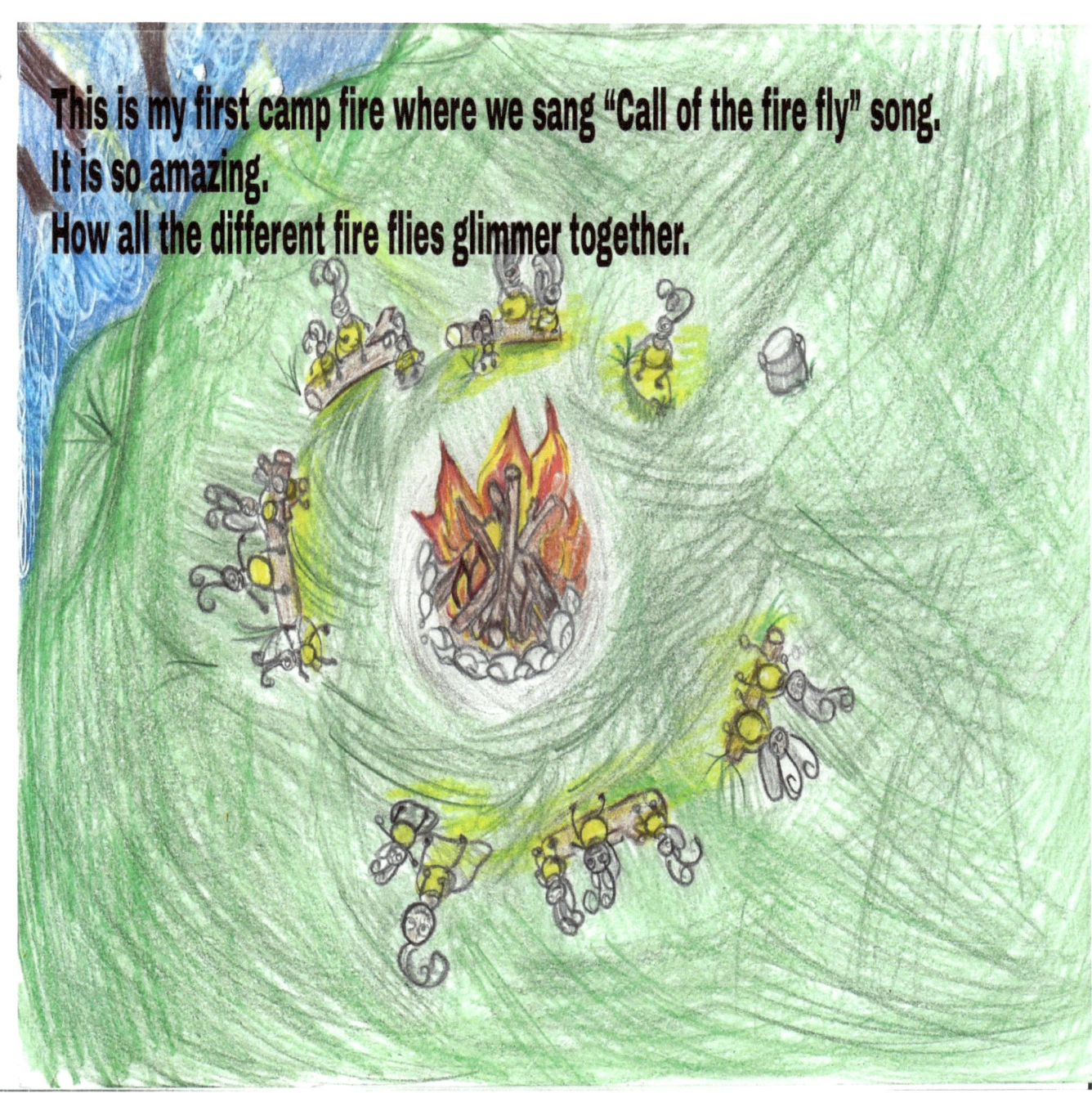

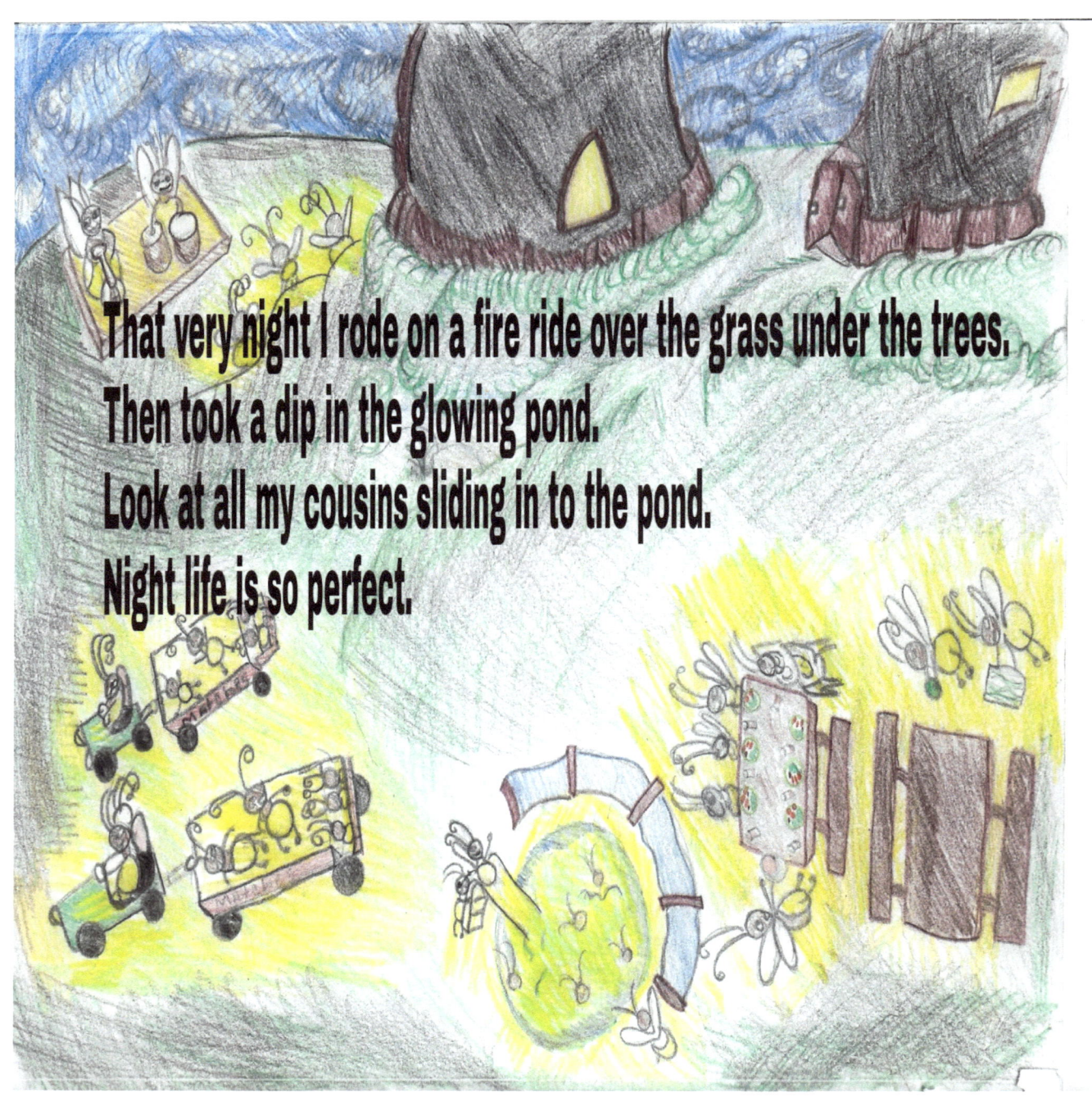

That very night I rode on a fire ride over the grass under the trees.

Then took a dip in the glowing pond.

Look at all my cousins sliding in to the pond.

Night life is so perfect.

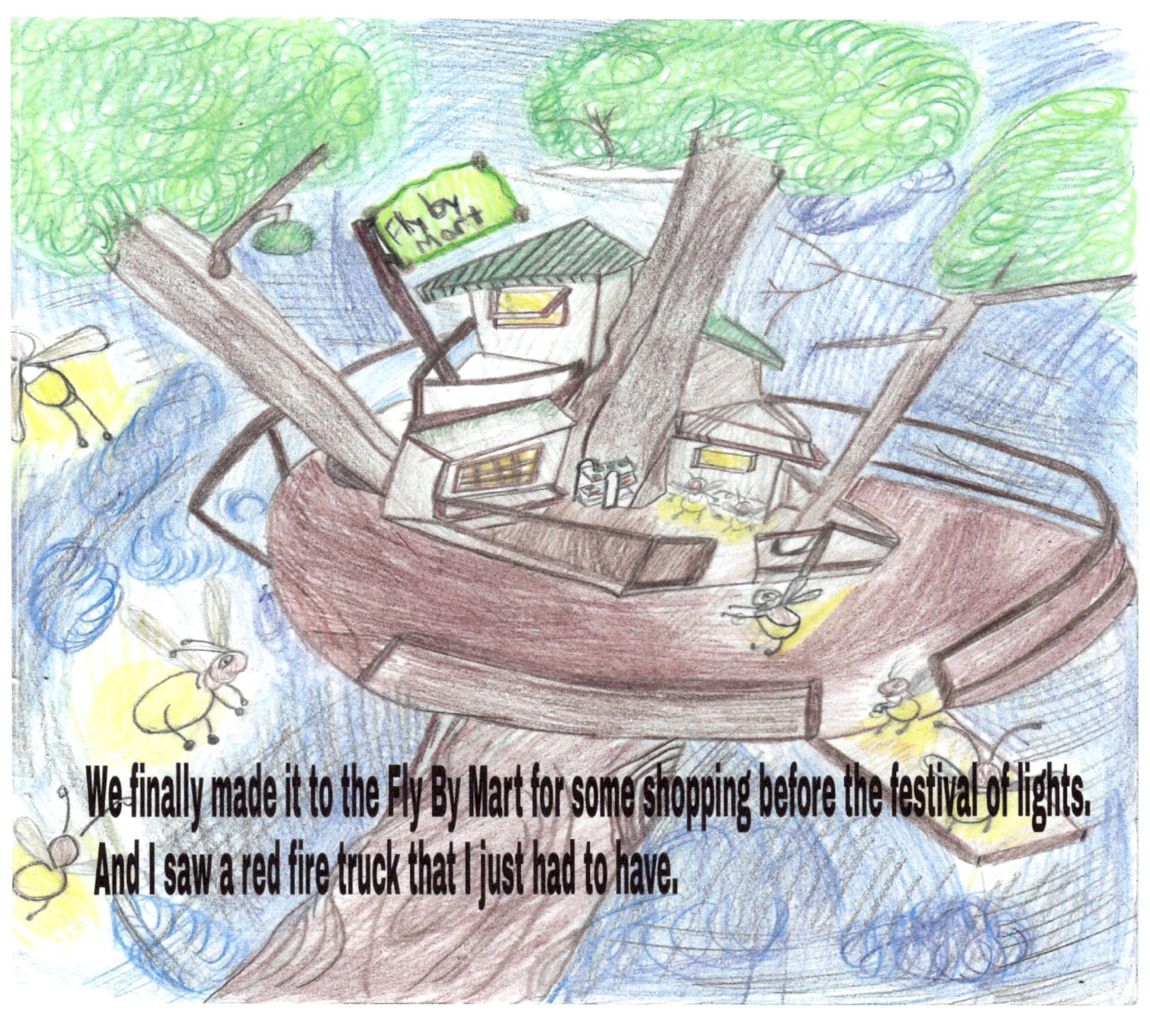

We finally made it to the Fly By Mart for some shopping before the festival of lights.
And I saw a red fire truck that I just had to have.

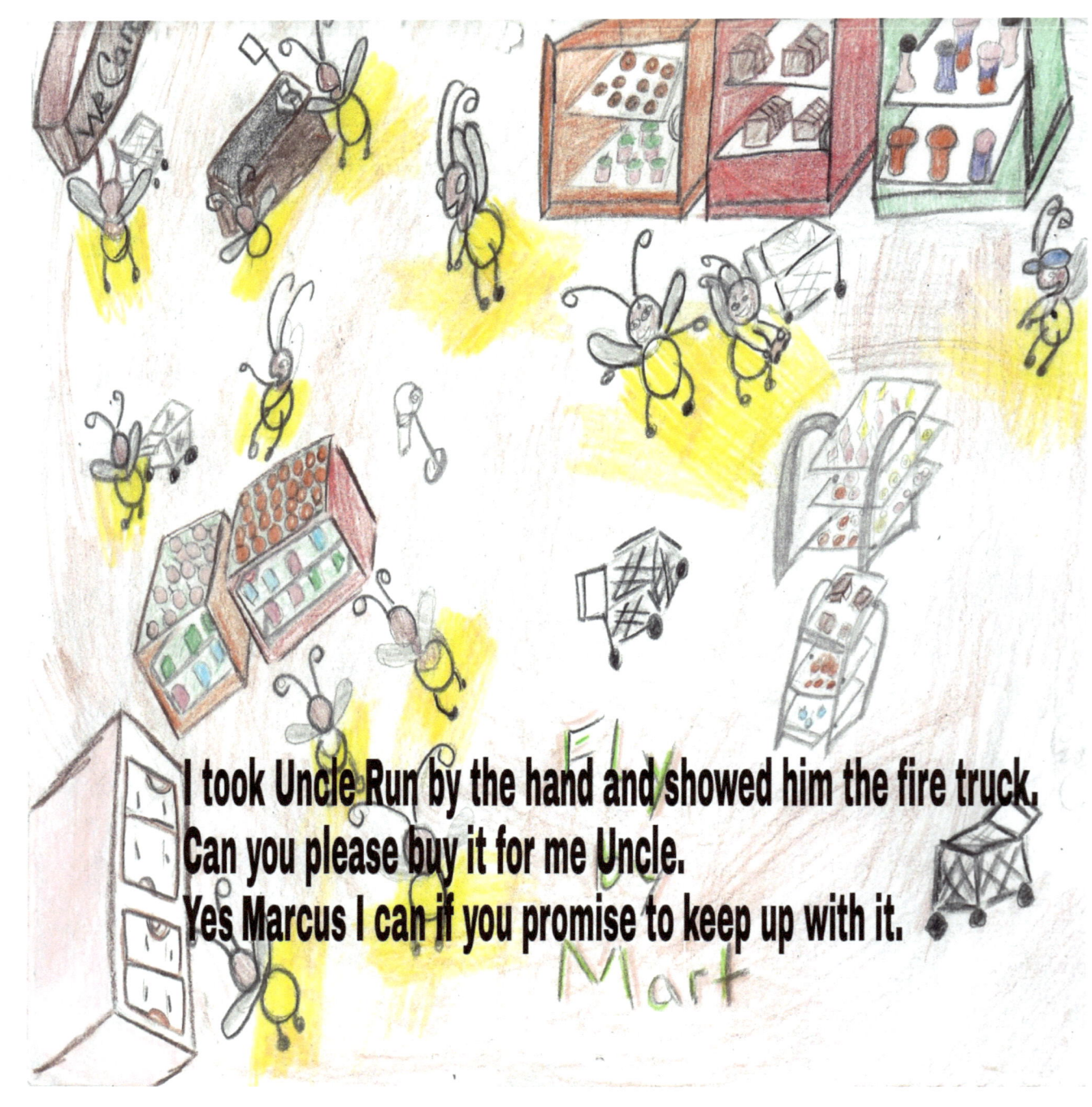

I took Uncle Run by the hand and showed him the fire truck.
Can you please buy it for me Uncle.
Yes Marcus I can if you promise to keep up with it.

Uncle Run had to take a nap after our long shopping trip.
I played with my fire truck.

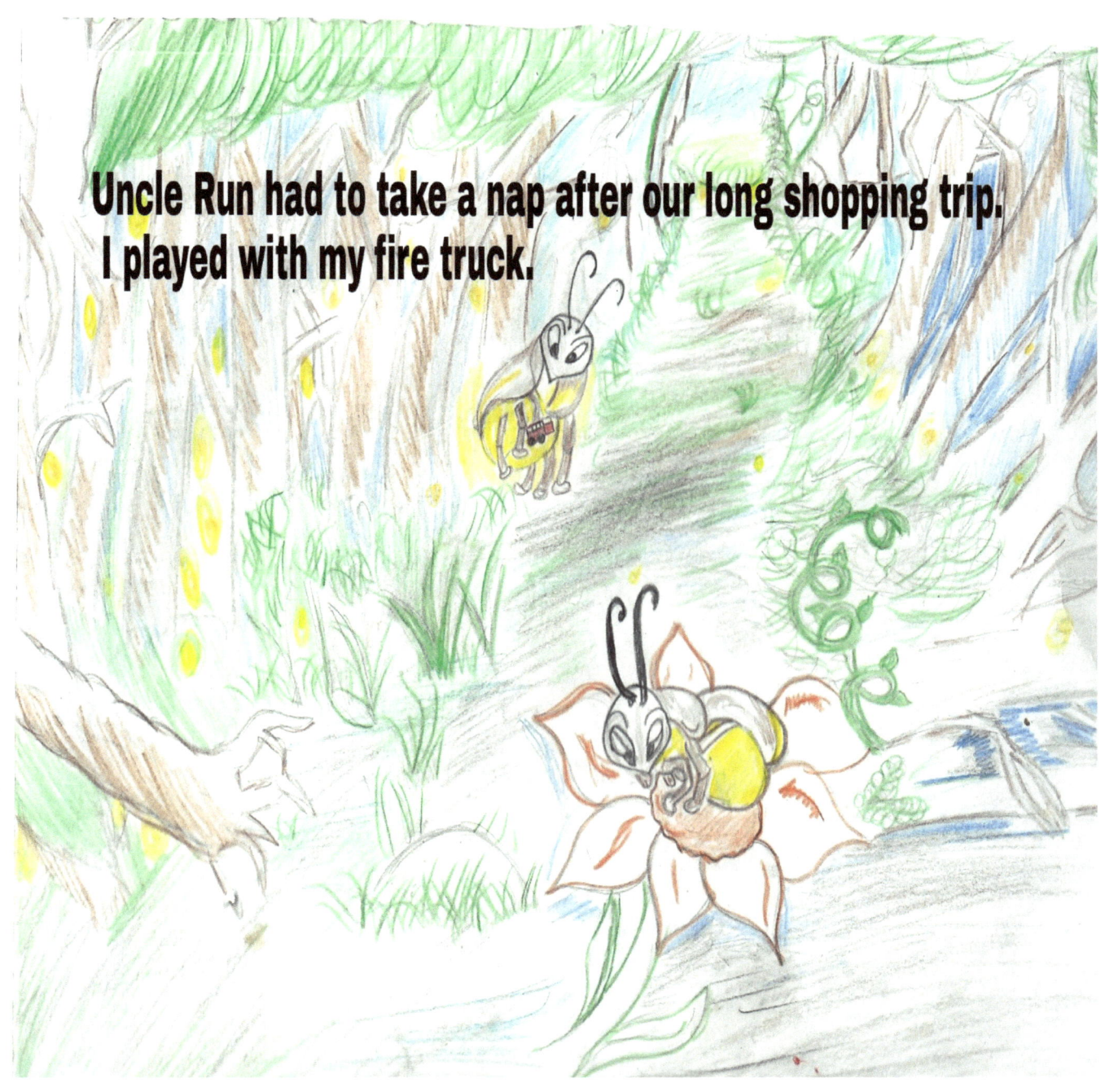

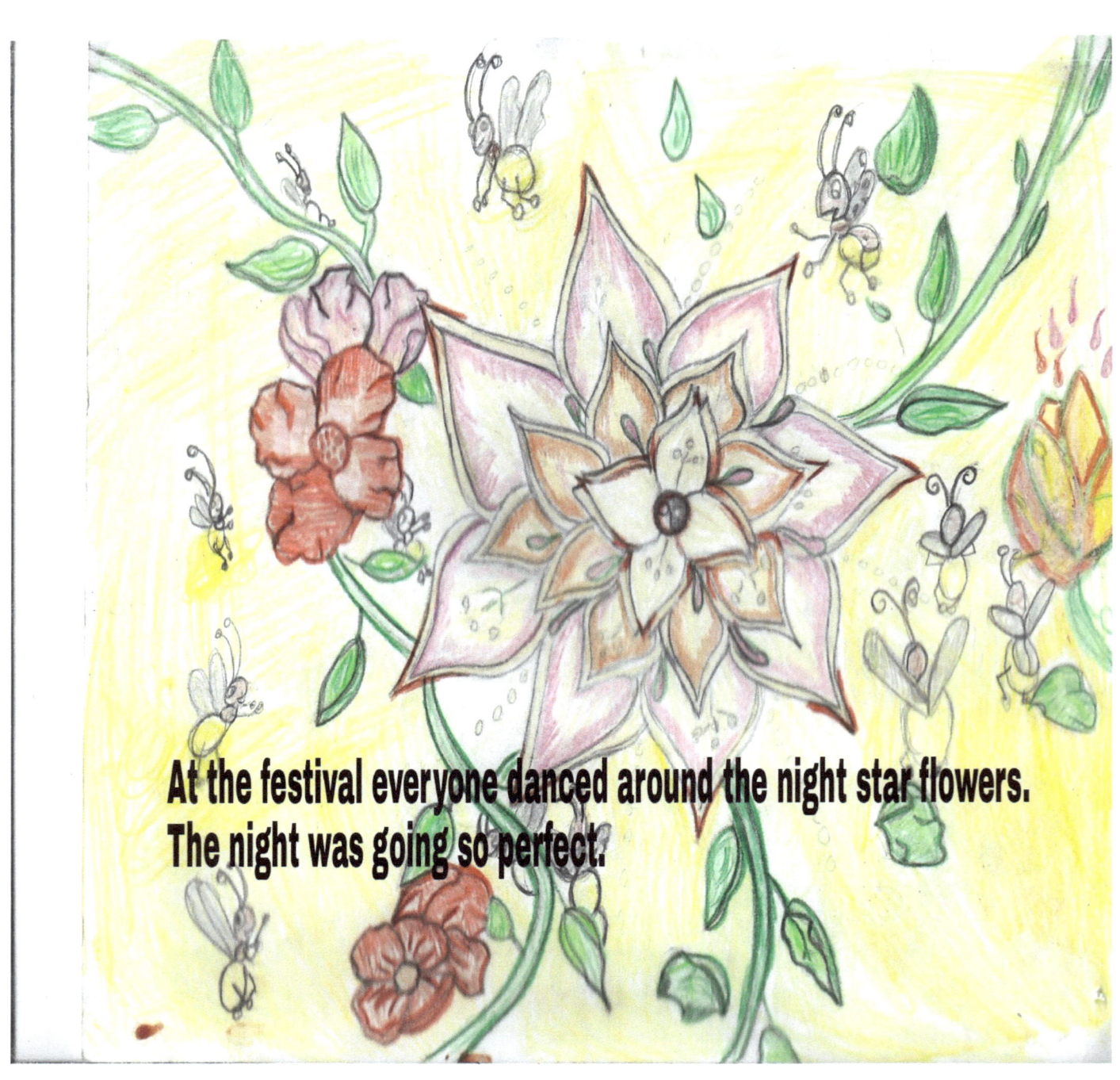

At the festival everyone danced around the night star flowers. The night was going so perfect.

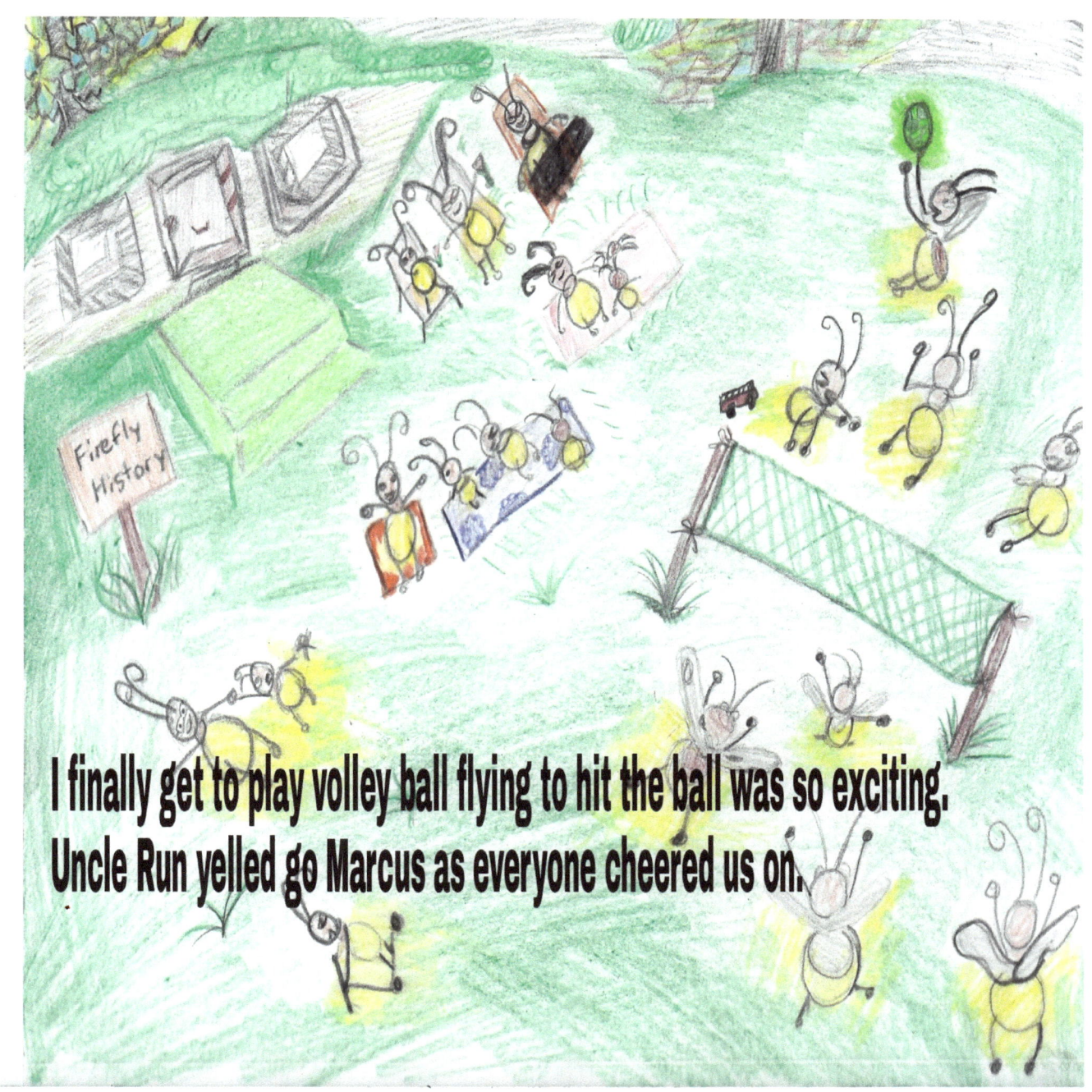

I finally get to play volley ball flying to hit the ball was so exciting. Uncle Run yelled go Marcus as everyone cheered us on.

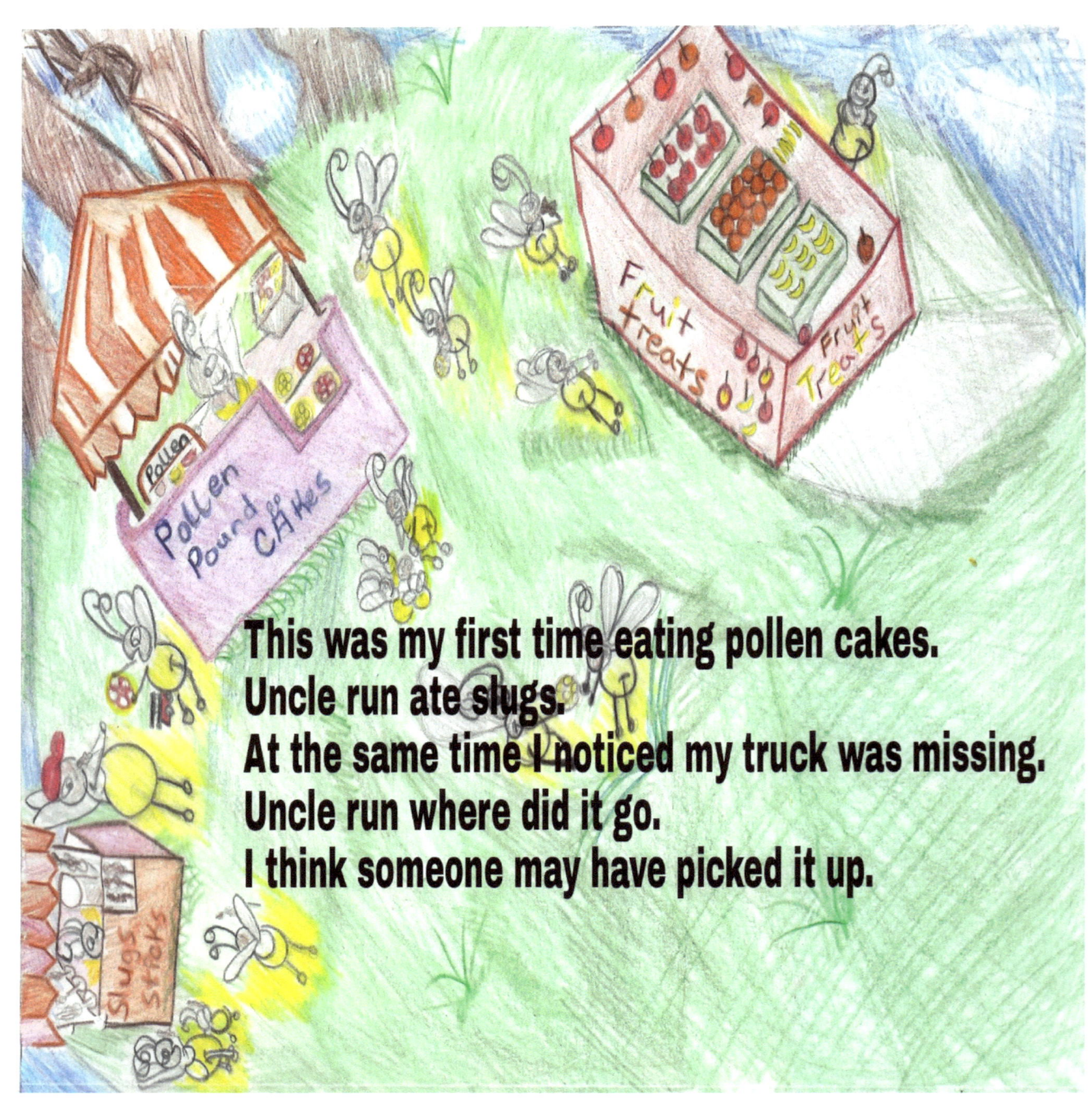

This was my first time eating pollen cakes.
Uncle run ate slugs.
At the same time I noticed my truck was missing.
Uncle run where did it go.
I think someone may have picked it up.

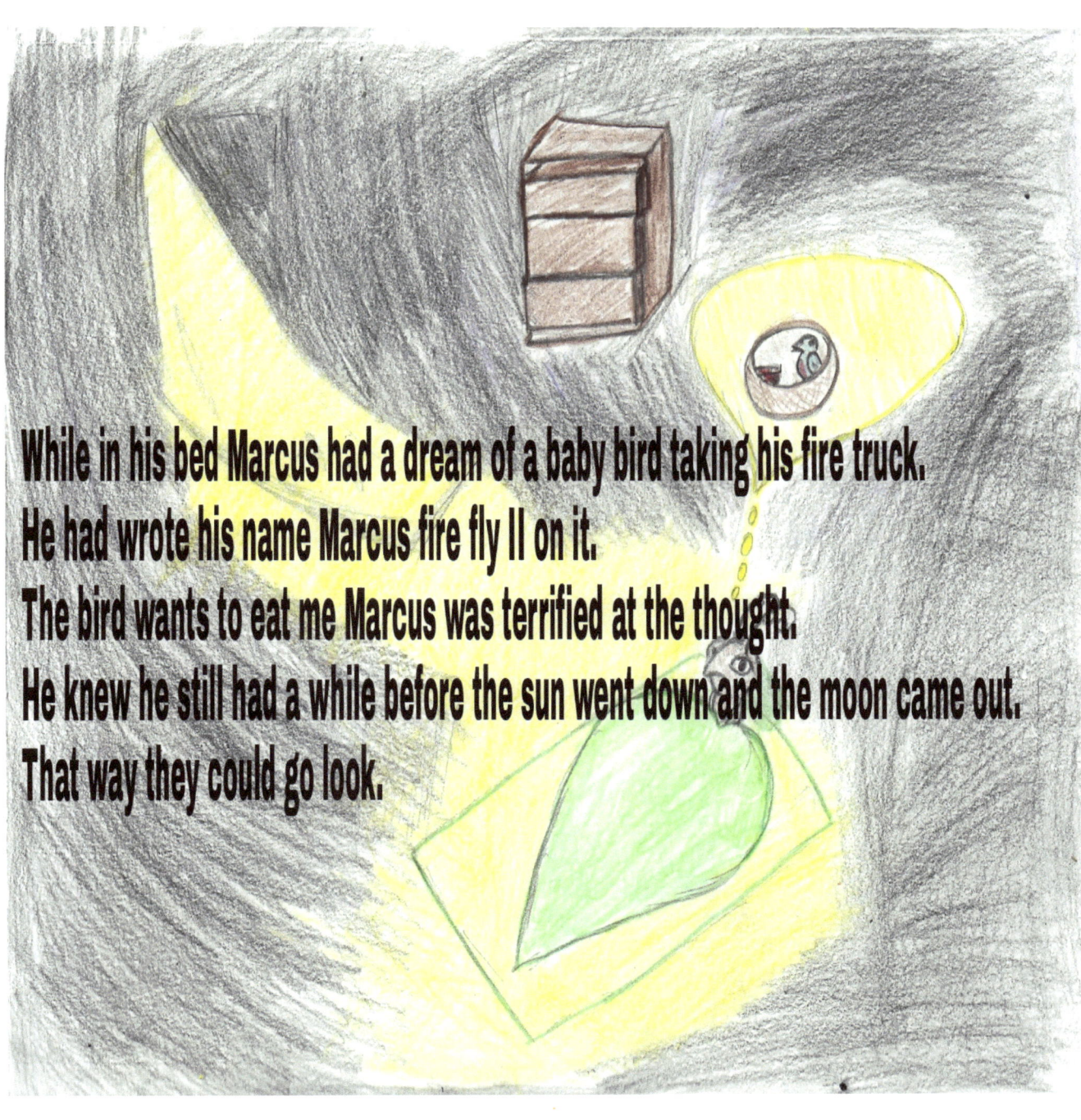

While in his bed Marcus had a dream of a baby bird taking his fire truck.

He had wrote his name Marcus fire fly II on it.

The bird wants to eat me Marcus was terrified at the thought.

He knew he still had a while before the sun went down and the moon came out.

That way they could go look.

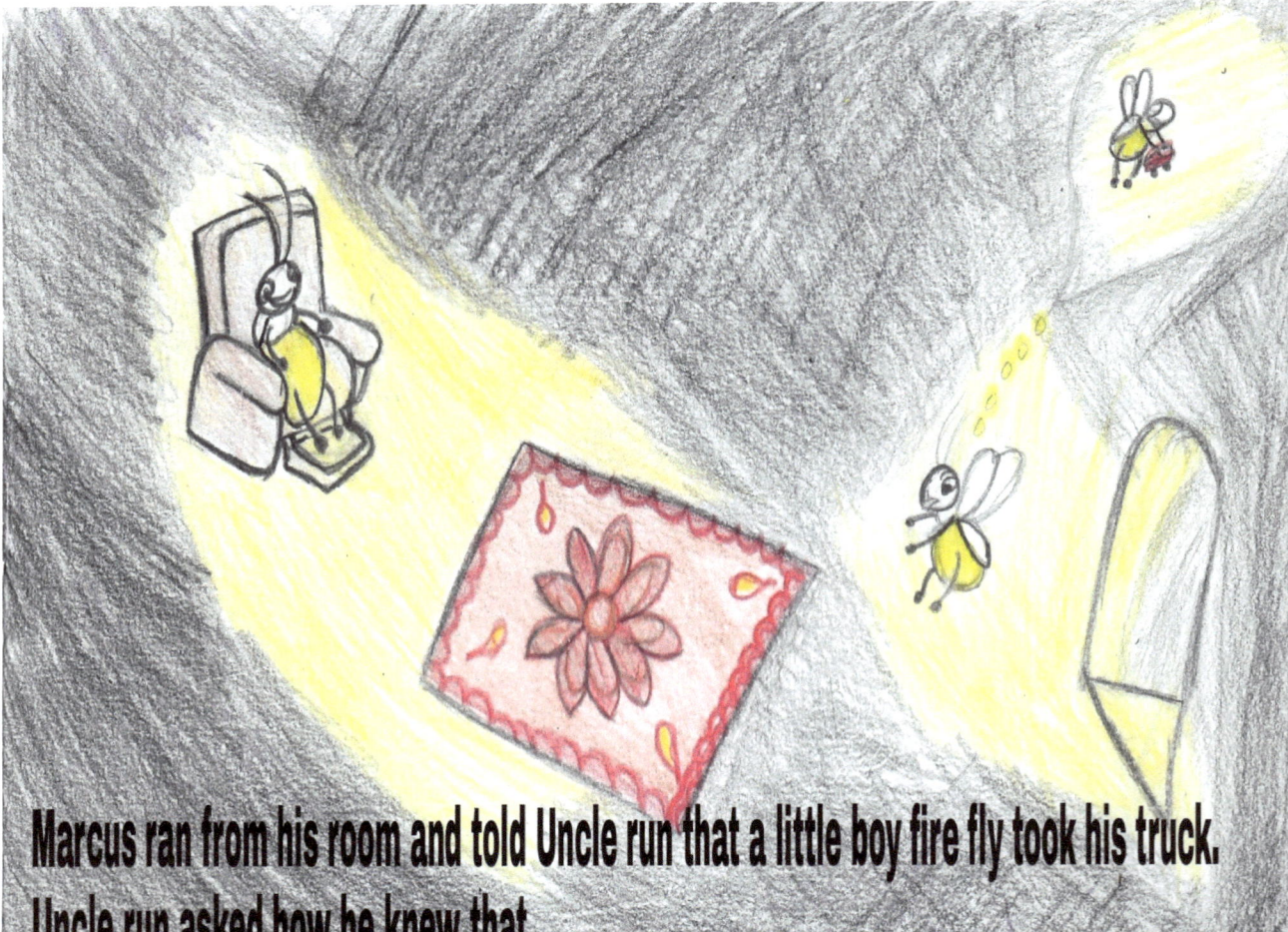

Marcus ran from his room and told Uncle run that a little boy fire fly took his truck.

Uncle run asked how he knew that.

Marcus said he saw it as clear as his light shines.

Someone has my fire truck Uncle run assured Marcus.

At first they would look for it when night came again.

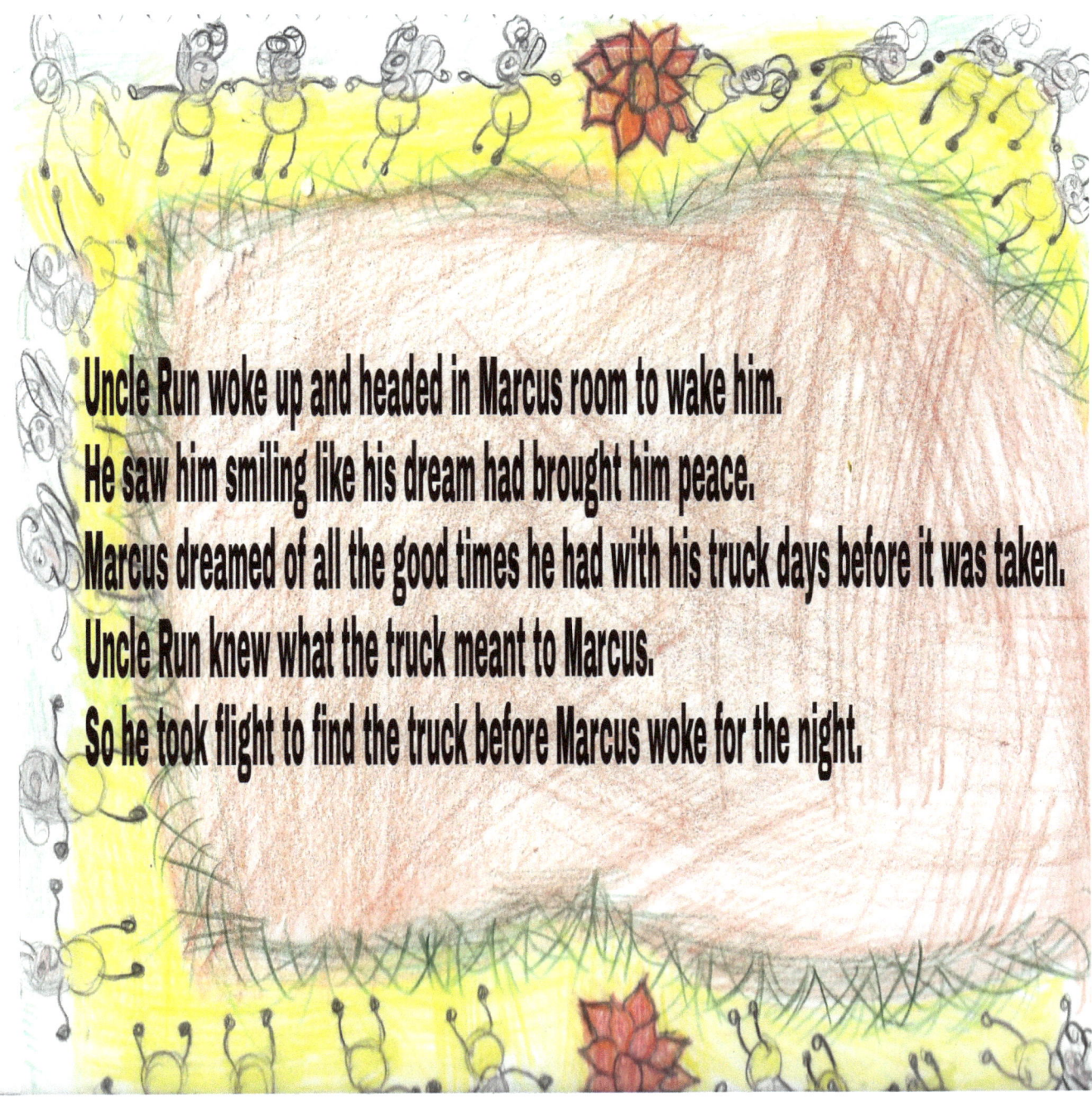

Uncle Run woke up and headed in Marcus room to wake him.

He saw him smiling like his dream had brought him peace.

Marcus dreamed of all the good times he had with his truck days before it was taken.

Uncle Run knew what the truck meant to Marcus.

So he took flight to find the truck before Marcus woke for the night.

Uncle showed up at the festival ground
and every thing was gone so he shinned his light
towards the bottom of the trees deep in the grass.
He saw a glimmer of light in the distance and went closer to see.
Who or what was shinning and there was the fire truck.
Uncle run was so excited he took flight back to the tree
house to wake Marcus and show him what he found.

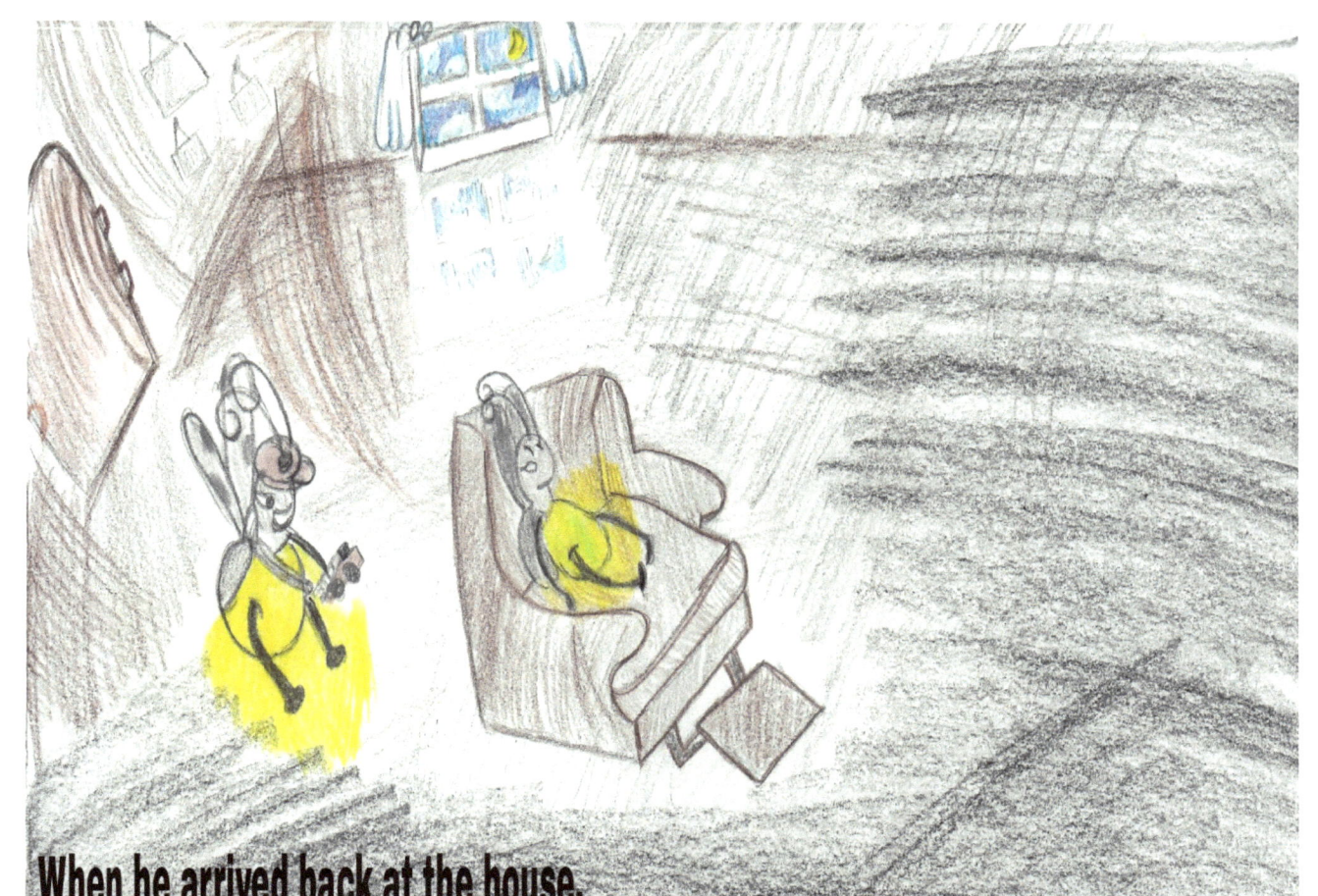

When he arrived back at the house.

He saw Marcus in his chair sleeping he sat the fire truck in his lap.

And called Marcus name to wake him.

Marcus jumped up and said Uncle Run we have to go look.

Marcus got really quiet when he saw the fire truck in his lap and was so happy.

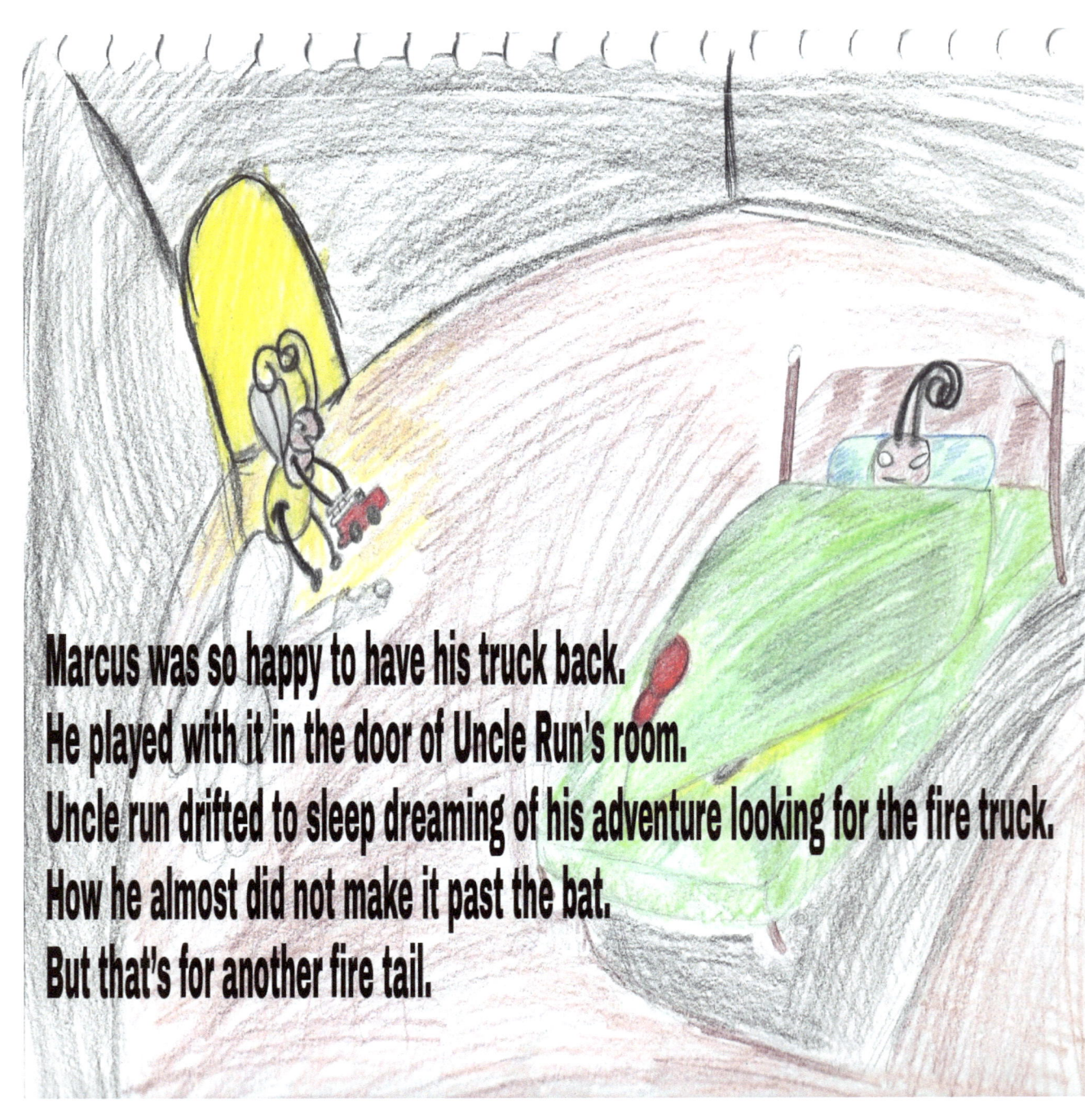

Marcus was so happy to have his truck back.

He played with it in the door of Uncle Run's room.

Uncle run drifted to sleep dreaming of his adventure looking for the fire truck.

How he almost did not make it past the bat.

But that's for another fire tail.

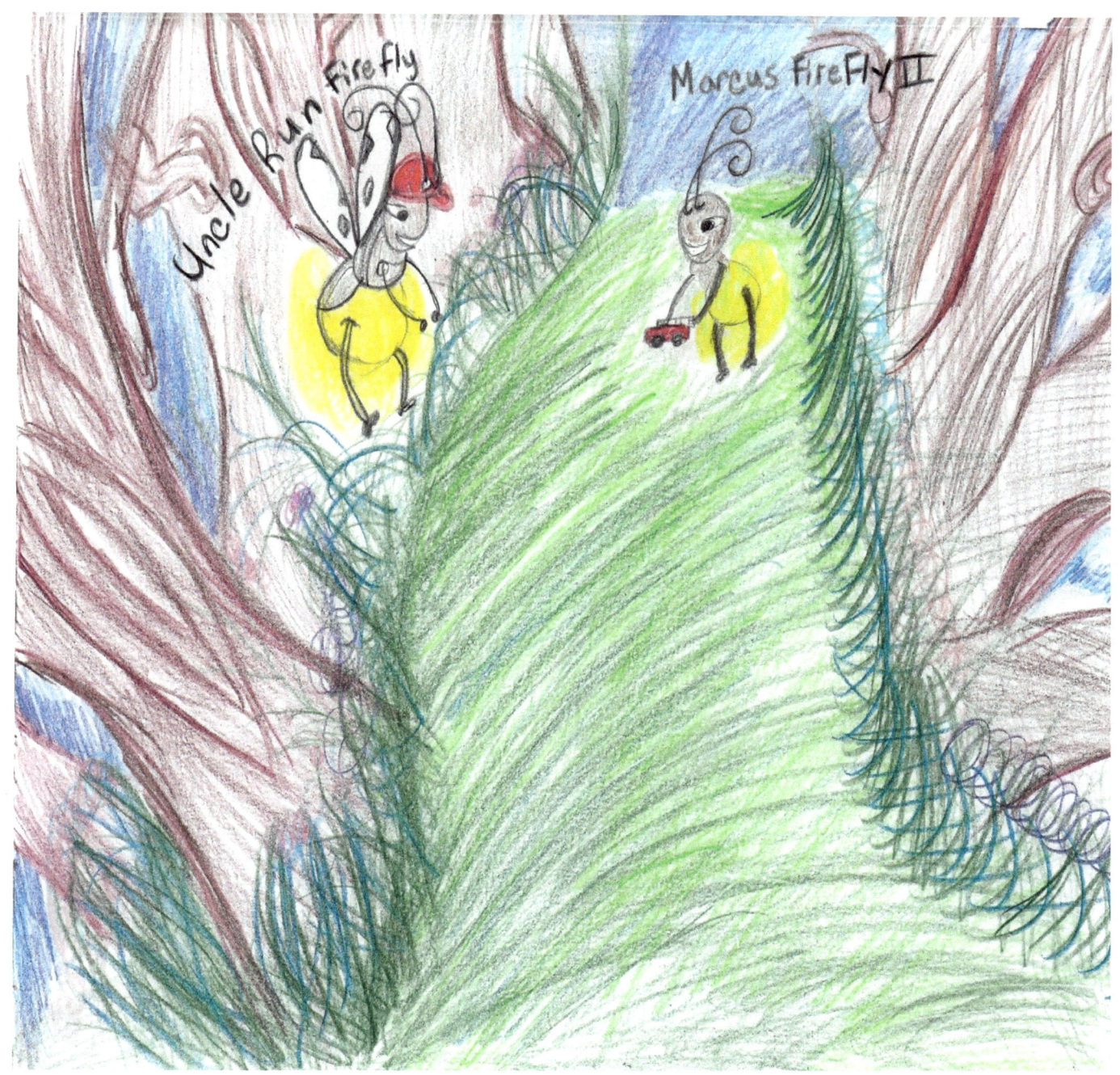

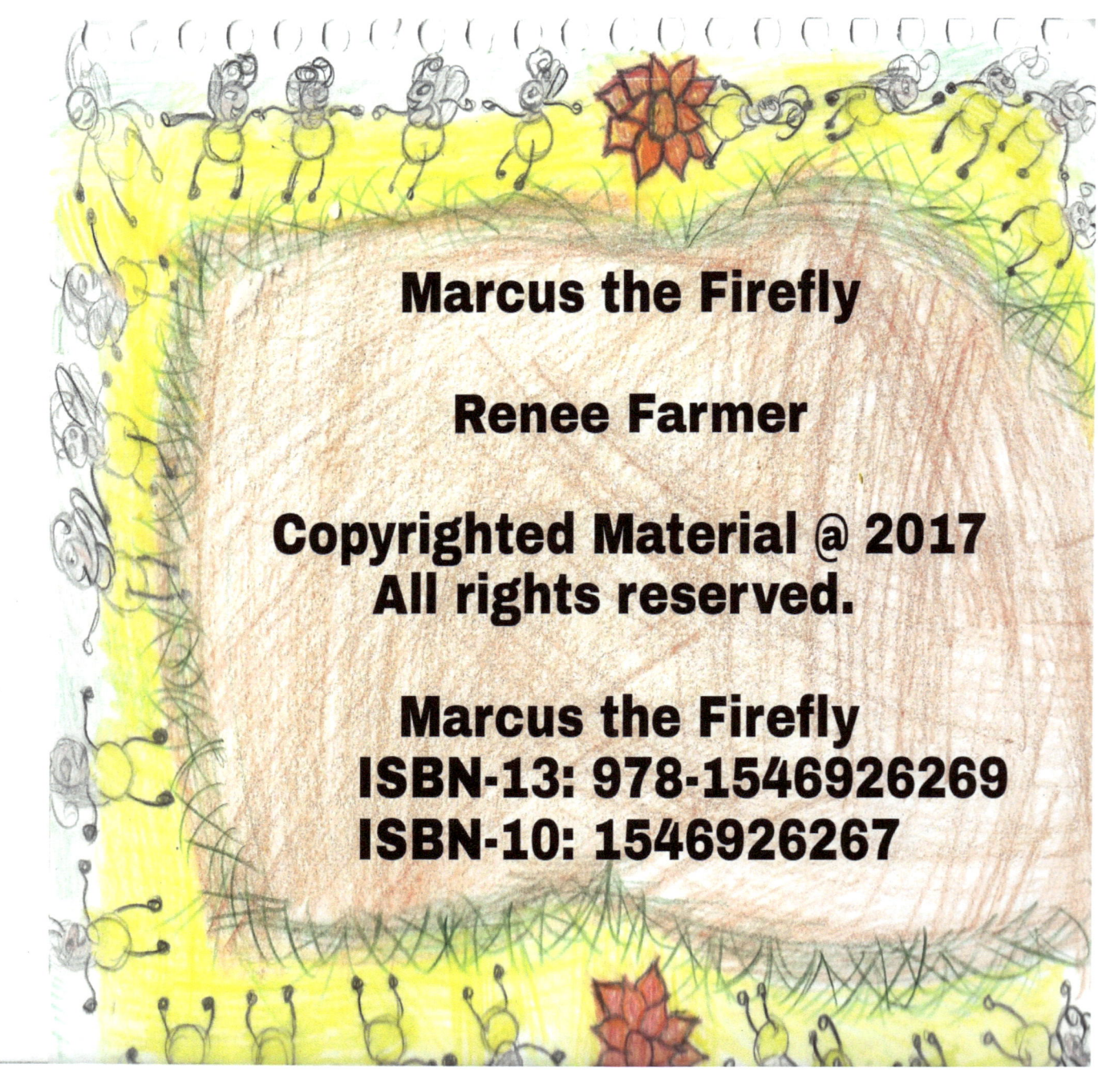

Marcus the Firefly

Renee Farmer

Marcus the Firefly
ISBN-13: 978-1546926269
ISBN-10: 1546926267

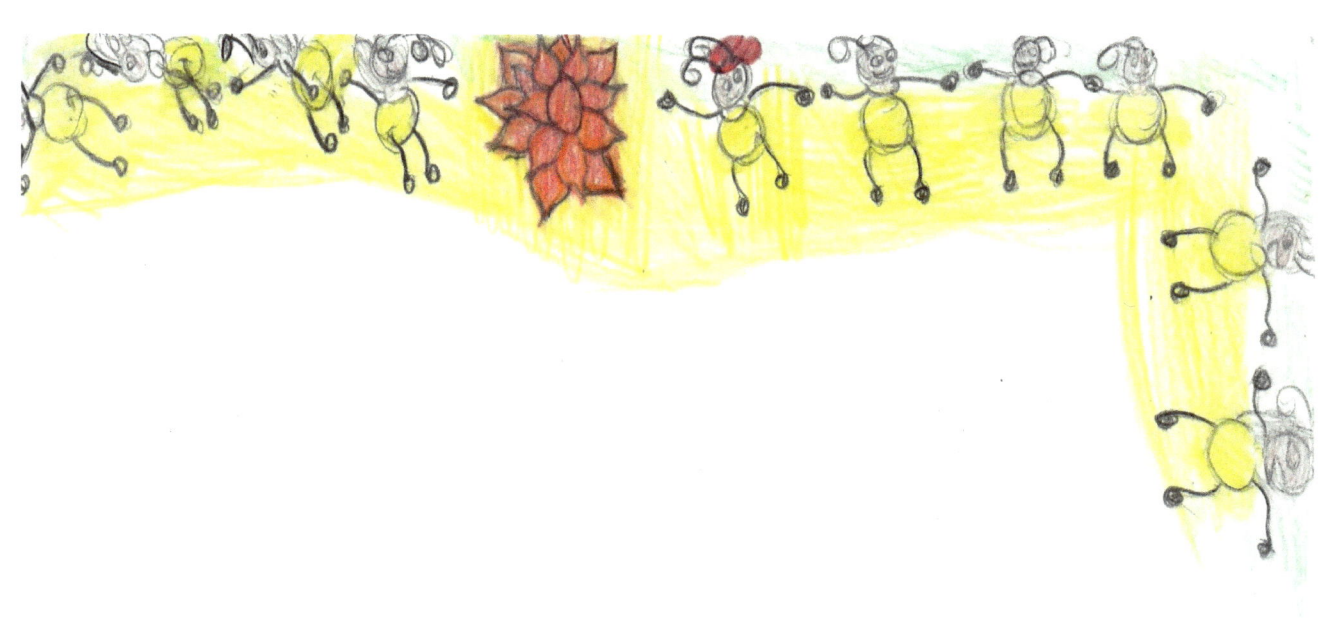
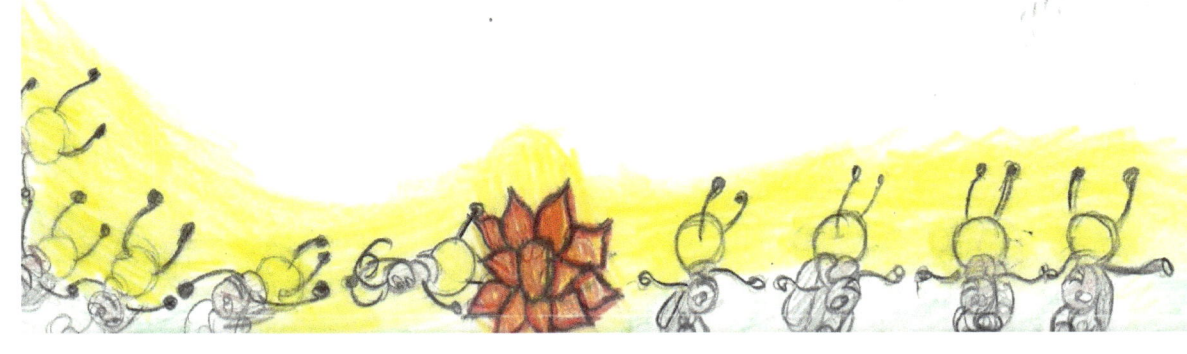

www.ingramcontent.com/pod-product-compliance
Lightning Source LLC
Chambersburg PA
CBHW041308180526
45172CB00003B/1021